Dear Parent:
Your child's love of reading starts here!

Every child learns to read in a different way and at his or her own speed. Some go back and forth between reading levels and read favorite books again and again. Others read through each level in order. You can help your young reader improve and become more confident by encouraging his or her own interests and abilities. From books your child reads with you to the first books he or she reads alone, there are I Can Read Books for every stage of reading:

SHARED READING
Basic language, word repetition, and whimsical illustrations, ideal for sharing with your emergent reader

BEGINNING READING
Short sentences, familiar words, and simple concepts for children eager to read on their own

READING WITH HELP
Engaging stories, longer sentences, and language play for developing readers

READING ALONE
Complex plots, challenging vocabulary, and high-interest topics for the independent reader

I Can Read Books have introduced children to the joy of reading since 1957. Featuring award-winning authors and illustrators and a fabulous cast of beloved characters, I Can Read Books set the standard for beginning readers.

A lifetime of discovery begins with the magical words **"I Can Read!"**

Visit www.icanread.com for information
on enriching your child's reading experience.

To great teachers
everywhere
—S. A.

To Manolo, Carmina, and
Gloria Sánchez Vega
—G. M.

Picture Credits
Photographs © Getty Images: page 28, Helen Keller feeling the face of Anne Sullivan, by Rolls Press/ Popperfoto; the graduation photo of Helen Keller, by Topical Press Agency; page 29, Helen Keller with Anne Sullivan, by Bettmann; Helen Keller with President Kennedy, by Historical; page 30, Helen Keller sitting at a desk, by Bettmann; page 31, Helen Keller, Jo Davidson, and Ernie Pyle, by Alfred Eisenstaedt; Helen Keller playing chess with Anne Sullivan Macy, by Bettmann, used courtesy of the American Foundation for the Blind via UPI; Helen Keller with Rt. Hon. W. Paling, by Topical Press Agency/Stringer; page 32, photo of Helen Keller, by Bettmann.

I Can Read® and I Can Read Book® are trademarks of HarperCollins Publishers.

Library of Congress Control Number: 2018961832
ISBN 978-0-06-243282-7 (trade bdg.)—ISBN 978-0-06-243281-0 (pbk.)

Book design by Marisa Rother
21 CWM 10 9 8 7 6
❖   First Edition

HELEN KELLER
The World at Her Fingertips

by Sarah Albee
pictures by Gustavo Mazali

HARPER
An Imprint of HarperCollinsPublishers

Helen Keller could not see.

She could not hear.

She could hardly speak.

But she learned to read and write.

She loved to swim and ride bikes.

Helen traveled all over the world.

She met twelve US presidents.

She spent her life helping others.

How did she do it?

Helen had been born healthy.
At six months, the happy baby
could even say a few words.

But when Helen was not yet two,

she got very sick with a high fever.

Baby Helen recovered at last.

But then her parents realized

she could no longer see or hear.

Helen's world became

dark and silent.

Little Helen could no longer speak.

Because she could not hear,

she forgot all her words.

She grew incredibly frustrated.

Helen screamed and kicked and hit.

Many people told her parents

that Helen would never learn.

They said Helen should be sent away.

Helen's parents refused.

Helen's parents wrote to a school
for blind people to ask for help.
The school sent a young woman
to their house to teach Helen.
Her name was Anne Sullivan.

Helen was nearly seven years old.

Anne was only twenty.

She came from a poor family.

She had very bad eyesight herself.

Helen's family had always let Helen

have her own way.

But Anne did not.

Anne was kind to Helen, but firm.

Anne made Helen eat with a spoon
and not with her fingers.

Helen threw her spoon on the floor.

Anne made her pick it up.

Helen shrieked and fought.

Anne remained firm.

Anne tried to teach Helen

to understand words and language.

Anne handed Helen a doll.

With her fingers,

Anne spelled D-O-L-L

in Helen's open hand.

Helen did not understand.

Anne kept trying.

And then one day, it worked.

Anne pumped water over Helen's hand.

Anne spelled out W-A-T-E-R.

In a flash, Helen understood.

Helen realized that Anne's fingers spelled words that named things. She zoomed from object to object. That day she learned F-A-T-H-E-R, M-O-T-H-E-R, and S-I-S-T-E-R. Anne was T-E-A-C-H-E-R.

Then Helen learned to read

by touching raised dots on a page.

Helen was the first blind and deaf

person to learn to read.

Newspapers printed stories

about Helen and Anne.

The two became famous.

Helen's world was now a happy place.

Helen was a brilliant student.

And Anne was a brilliant teacher.

Anne lived at their home for years.

Helen learned to read lips.

Helen got into Radcliffe College.

Anne went with her to help her.

While still in college,

Helen wrote a book about her life.

After college, Helen kept writing.

"We are never really happy
until we try to brighten
the lives of others," Helen said.
She helped the poor.
She helped children.

Helen also helped women
win the right to vote.
Anne was always at her side.

But Anne's eyesight was fading.

And Anne's health was failing.

Helen needed more help.

Helen hired a housekeeper.
Her name was Polly Thomson.
She learned how to help Helen
with reading and with travel.
She became a close friend.

For years, the three lived together.

Then, in 1936, Anne died.

Anne had been Helen's teacher

for almost fifty years.

Helen missed her friend.

But she and Polly kept working.

Helen raised money for the blind.

She comforted injured soldiers.

Helen loved to smell flowers,

to cuddle dogs, to taste good food,

to "feel" music, and to "touch" art.

Helen loved life.

Helen changed the way the world
viewed deaf and blind people.
She inspired deaf and blind people
to believe in themselves.
She lived a full life
with courage and with joy.

Timeline

1840

1850

1860

1870

1880

1890

1900

1880
Helen Keller is born in
Tuscumbia, Alabama,
on June 27.

1882
At nineteen months of age, Helen
Keller is struck with a high fever. She
loses her sight and her hearing.

1887
In March, teacher
Anne Sullivan arrives at
the Kellers' home.

In April, Keller learns that
objects have names.

In July, Keller begins to
learn Braille.

1900
Keller enrolls at
Radcliffe College.

1903
Helen Keller's first book is published,
called *The Story of My Life*.

1900

1904

Helen Keller
graduates from
Radcliffe.

1910

1920

1914

Polly Thomson comes to
work with Helen and Anne.

1930

1936

Anne Sullivan dies.

1940

1960

Helen Keller meets
President Kennedy.
He's the twelfth US
president she meets.

Polly Thomson dies.

1950

1960

1968

Helen Keller dies at age
eighty-seven on June 1.

Reading

With Braille (BRAYL), Helen could read. Braille is a way of printing for blind people. Raised dots represent letters of the alphabet. A blind person can "read" with her fingers. The system was invented in 1824 by a man named Louis Braille, who had been blind since the age of three.

Braille

Here is how you spell Helen's first name in Braille:

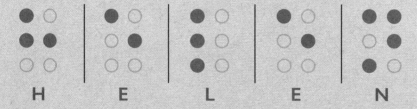

H   E   L   E   N

Here is the alphabet in Braille. Can you spell your own name?

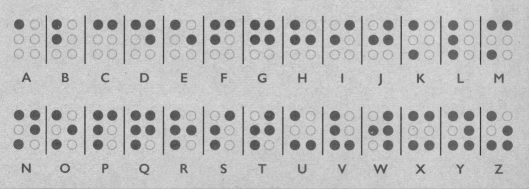

A B C D E F G H I J K L M

N O P Q R S T U V W X Y Z